WRITE FASTER:

Proven Methods to Increase Your Writing Speed and Efficiency

Tarannum Khan

Struggling with incomplete exam papers and slow notes writing?

Don't let your grades suffer...

Discover the secret to speedwriting today!

In just 15 minutes of training, watch your writing speed soar.

Start now and track your progress from the first stroke to the final line!"

Note: These activities can be done under supervision for small kids and can be self-guided for elders or teenagers, by keeping track of your progress honestly in the provided table as we unleash the power of speedwriting together.

Contents

Activity 1:
Initial Pace

Before you start the training, copy the lines given below in a notebook at your current speed.

As you start…set a timer to 1 minute and start copying the lines, on the count of 1 minute…stop!

Enlightened as stars, I fly so high,

With feathers on my back,

That no one can deny…

My loved ones thought,

I will rage the sky,

But there was a time, when I couldn't fly…

As minds around me,

Filled with orthodox thoughts,

Would pull down my strings,

As and when they thought…!

But alas! No one could seize,

When I took a flight, in my dream!

And count the number of alphabets written ____

This is your current speed per minute

(Enter it in Activity 1 column in the table below)

Activity 1 Initial time	Activity 2	Activity 3	Activity 4			Activity 5			Activity 6	Activity 7	Activity 8	Final Activity 9
___letters/ min			A1	A2	A3	B1	B2	B3				

Goal: To reach more number of alphabets in same amount of time!

Before diving into the secret, let's set the stage with some crucial tips:

1. Opt for a lightweight pen without a cap to minimize any added weight though in milligrams, as it can hinder your speed.

2. Keep your grip light to conserve energy and prevent early fatigue, ensuring you can finish your notes or exams without struggle.

3. Do not compromise with your handwriting for writing fast. To ensure this we must first ensure improving the handwriting and then going for speed writing practice, following the directions and preserving the handwriting quality at every point.

4. Avoid writing too big letters, they will take more time… on the contrary it doesn't mean writing too small to save time, as Clarity is key for easy reading. This will save time for both you and your examiner, in turn help you score better marks.

Ready to unlock the ultimate speedwriting technique? Let's get started! with activity 2

Activity 2:
Pangram Writing

Rewrite the provided pangram as many times as possible in one minute, in your regular handwriting.

What does a Pangram mean? In simple terms, a pangram is a sentence in which every alphabet occur at least once. It is like a special sentence that includes all the letters from a to z

Set a stopwatch for 1 minute and start writing the line. Repeat writing the line again and again until the minute is up.

'The quick brown fox jumps over the lazy dog.'

Stop exactly at the end of 1 minute, count the total number of alphabets written and enter it in column Activity 2 column.

Activity 1 Initial time	Activity 2 Pangram	Activity 3	Activity 4			Activity 5			Activity 6	Activity 7	Activity 8	Final Activity 9
			A1	A2	A3	B1	B2	B3				
	__letters/ min											

As we proceed, have a reality check, are you are holding the Pen/Pencil properly –

If NOT? Then it can be achieved by following the **Dynamic Tripod technique**

But what is it?

The dynamic tripod technique refers to a grasp pattern used primarily in writing and fine motor activities. It involves holding an object, such as a pen or pencil, with three fingers: the thumb, index finger, and middle finger. This technique allows for greater control, precision, and flexibility in movement.

Position your fingers according to Dynamic Tripod technique:

1. Thumb: Positioned against the side of the index finger, providing stability.
2. Index Finger: Positioned on top of the pen or pencil, applying downward pressure.
3. Middle Finger: Supports the pen or pencil from below, providing balance and additional control.
4. Ring and Little Fingers: Generally curled into the palm, not actively involved in holding the pen or pencil but can provide additional stability.

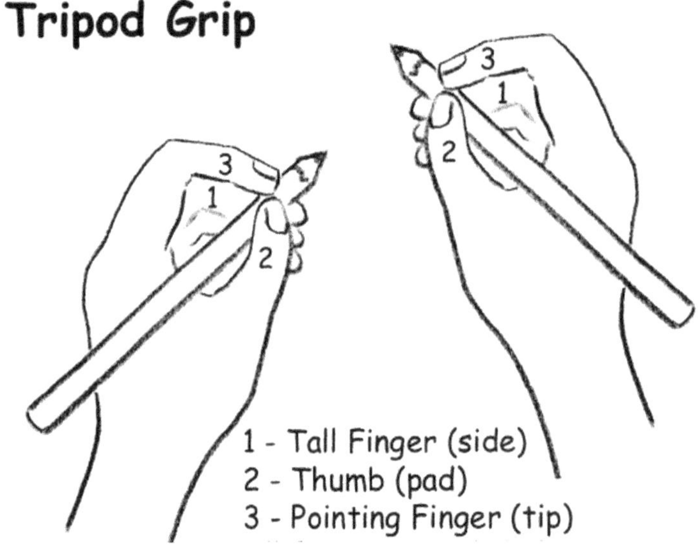

Benefits:

➢ **Improved Control**: The dynamic tripod grasp allows for small, precise movements, which is essential for legible handwriting.

➢ **Reduced Fatigue**: This grip is efficient, reducing strain and fatigue during prolonged writing tasks.

➢ **Enhanced Proficiency**: It allows for quick and varied finger movements, making it suitable for detailed work.

Now, let's take it a step further with activity 3

Activity 3:
Alphabet Flow

In this activity write the letters from a to z with pen or pencil, continuously (as shown below) repeating the sequence, once over. Repeat it as many times as you can write within one minute.

Write in the font you are generally use to, that is cursive or block letters (also known as print letters)

Set your timer for 1 minute.

Abcdefghijklmnopqrstuvwxyz (cursive- small case)

Or

abcdefghijklmnopqrstuvwxyz (block or print letters - small case)

Stop writing as the timer expires.

Count the number of alphabets written at the end of 1 minute

Alphabets in one minute _____ (Record this count in Activity 3 column of the table)

Activity 1 Initial time	Activity 2 Pangram	Activity 3 Alphabet Flow	Activity 4			Activity 5			Activity 6	Activity 7	Activity 8	Final Activity 9
		__letters/ min	A1	A2	A3	B1	B2	B3				

Additional Factors that promotes speed writing

In order to write fast we need to train our hand muscles for same , just like how athlete train their body muscles to run faster and build stamina. We can also take an example of people who are performing daily workouts, when workout is done occasionally, it causes cramps and lot of body pain but by doing it regularly, the body gets use to it and makes it simpler. Similar logic holds true for training hand muscles too for writing. So below given are some exercising tips to train hand muscles for speed writing:-

1. Squeeze a soft ball 5-6 times to free your hand muscles.

2. Take about 10-15 coins and pick them individually from one place and shift to another place, as quick as possible, to increase fine motor skills.

3. Make some paper balls using waste paper. This exercise involves precise hand movements like squeezing and crumpling the paper, which strengthens the small muscles in the hands and fingers.

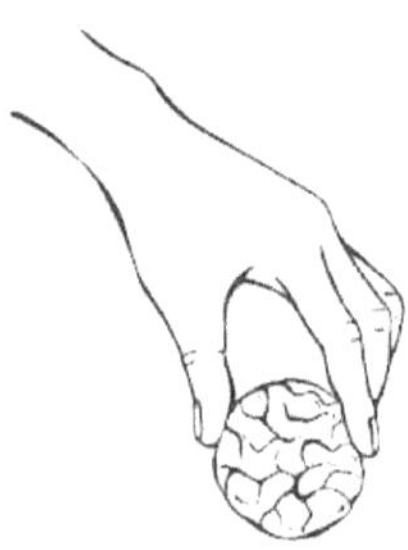

4. Move your fingers run up and down on pencil (holding the pencil in writing position), as fast as you can. This exercise if performed regularly gives strength to finger muscles, improves overall control, making it easier to perform task related to writing.

5. Place a rubber band around fingers, stretch the fingers out and relax, repeat about 7-8 times. This exercise will be particularly effective to improve finger flexibility, for improving grip strength, and working on overall hand endurance.

Activity 4:

Air brushing…

What is **Air brushing**???

Air Brushing is controlling the pressure and movement of the writing to achieve a consistent and graceful flow.

How to conduct this activity: Take your index finger in air and just randomly make shapes of letters from a to z (not too big neither too small) **in air**

Abcdefghijklmnopqrstuvwxyz (cursive- small case)

Or

Abcdefghijklmnopqrstuvwxyz (Block or print letters – lower case)

When airbrushing with your right hand, support your right elbow with your left palm. Conversely, if you are airbrushing with your left hand, support your left elbow with your right palm. This support helps stabilize your hand and provides better control over your movements, resulting in more precise and consistent airbrushing.

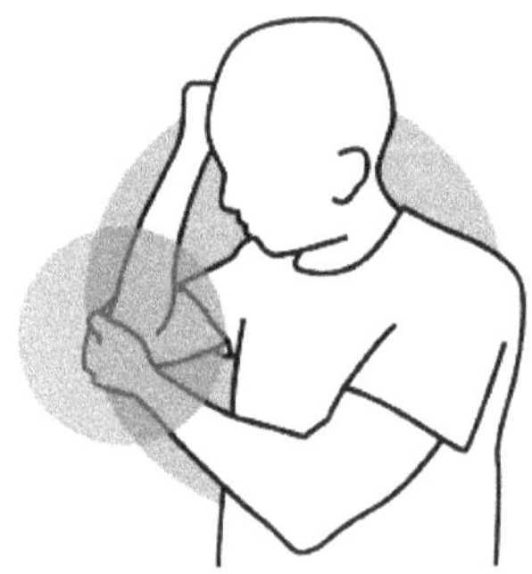

Practice once ....

Start the stopwatch as you begin writing from A in air, and stop it as you finish writing up to Z once.

Note the time taken _____ seconds and record it as A1 in the table.

Set the stop watch and note the time again by performing air brushing for second time, this time trying to speed up and achieve lesser time than A1.

Record this new time ____secs in A2 column of the table.

If the desired speed is not achieved in the second attempt, continue practicing and trying to speed up with each subsequent attempt. Note the time taken for each trial, recording them as A3, A4, A5, and so on, until the desired speed is attained

Note: Difference of even some seconds is considerable.

Activity 1 Initial time	Activity 2 Pangram	Activity 3 Alphabet Flow	Activity 4 Airbrushing			Activity 5			Activity 6	Activity 7	Activity 8	Final Activity 9
			A1	A2	A3	B1	B2	B3				
			__ secs	__ secs	__ secs							

Proceeding further with activity 5

Activity 5:
TABLE WRITING

Use your Index finger point (using your Index finger as pencil itself) and write a to z on table (not too big neither too small) just like average handwriting size that we use in notebook

Abcdefghijklmnopqrstuvwxyz
(cursive- small case)

Or

Abcdefghijklmnopqrstuvwxyz
(Print or Block letters- lower case)

Start the stopwatch as you begin writing from A on the table, and stop it as you finish writing up to Z once.

Note the time taken ____ seconds and record it as B1 in the table.

Set the stop watch and note the time again by performing Table writing for second time, this time trying to speed up and achieve lesser time than B1.

Record this new time ____secs in B2 column of the table.

If the desired speed is not achieved in the second attempt, continue practicing and trying to speed up with each subsequent attempt. Note the time taken for each trial, recording them as B3, B4, B5, and so on, until the desired speed is attained.

Note: Difference of even some seconds is considerable.

Activity 1 Initial time	Activity 2 Pangram	Activity 3 Alphabet Flow	Activity 4 Airbrushing			Activity 5 Table writing			Activity 6	Activity 7	Activity 8	Final Activity 9
			D1	D2	D3	B1	B2	B3				
						___ secs	___ secs	___ secs				

Activity 6:
Speed Pangram

This time write the provided pangram as many times as possible in one minute, ensuring better speed then activity 2, as our hand muscles have been trained a little for same by now.

Set a stopwatch for 1 minute and start writing the line. Repeat writing the line again and again until the minute is up.

' Rusqi pack my box with five dozen small jugs '

Stop exactly at the end of 1 minute, count the total number of alphabets written _____ and enter it in Activity 6 column.

Activity 1 Initial time	Activity 2 Pangram	Activity 3 Alphabet Flow	Activity 4 Airbrushing			Activity 5 Table writing			**Activity 6 Speed Pangram**	Activity 7	Activity 8	Final Activity 9
			A1	A2	A3	B1	B2	B3	___letters/ min			

Activity 7:
Speed writing challenge

Set the stop watch for 1 min, and start writing the lines below, as much as you can finish in 1 minutes.

Remember stop exactly at the end of 1 minute!

Enlightened as stars, I fly so high,

With feathers on my back,

That no one can deny…

My loved ones thought,

I will rage the sky,

But there was a time,

When I couldn't fly…

As minds around me,

Filled with orthodox thoughts,

Would pull down my strings,

As and when they thought…!

But alas! No one could seize,

When I took a flight, in my dream!

Count the number of alphabets written at the end of 1 minute____ and make a note in activity 7 column

Activity 1 Initial time	Activity 2 Pangram	Activity 3 Alphabet flow	Activity 4 Airbrushing			Activity 5 Table writing			Activity 6 Pangram	**Activity 7 Speed writing**	Activity 8	Final Activity 9
			A1	A2	A3	B1	B2	B3		__letters/ min		

You will Notice the number has increased as compared to Activity 1.

SO now what? ...this is the way to go ...Let's speed it up further with Activity 8

Activity 8:
A challenge to Activity 7!

Repeat writing the lines again (given in activity 7) trying to completing more number of lines than in activity 7, ensuring the neatness and clarity of writing.

Aim is to beat the speed achieved in activity 7 (by writing more number of alphabets in same time)

So set and start the stop watch and ...stop! As the minute ends!

Enlightened as stars, I fly so high,

With feathers on my back,

That no one can deny...

My loved ones thought,

I will rage the sky,

But there was a time,

When I couldn't fly...

As minds around me,

Filled with orthodox thoughts,

Would pull down my strings,

As and when they thought...!

But alas! No one could seize,

When I took a flight, in my dream!

Activity 1	Activity 2	Activity 3	Activity 4			Activity 5			Activity 6	Activity 7	**Activity 8**	Final Activity 9
Initial time	Pangram	Alphabet Flow	Airbrushing			Table writing			Speed Pangram	Speed Writing	**Challenge**	
			A1	A2	A3	B1	B2	B3			__letters / min	

Count the number of alphabets written at the end of 1 minute____ and make a note of it in Activity 8 column.

You will notice a little improvement than activity 7, may be of few seconds, but it is a positive sign of gaining speed, if not try it once again to achieve better number of letters in 1 minute.

Activity 9:
Jet speed

Finally it's time to put your best efforts and get the maximum number of letters written in 1 minute but remember the rule – No compromise on legibility and neatness of writing!

Set the stop watch for 1 minute, be ready to give your best …

Note: The purpose of writing same lines 3 times (in activity 7, 8 and 9) is to ensure speed on same number and pattern of letters, with a reduction of time in each trial, consecutively not compromising on handwriting neatness and legibility.

Enlightened as stars, I fly so high,

With feathers on my back,

That no one can deny…

My loved ones thought,

I will rage the sky,

But there was a time,

When I couldn't fly…

As minds around me,

Filled with orthodox thoughts,

Would pull down my strings,

As and when they thought…!

But alas! No one could seize,

When I took a flight, in my dream!

Finally make a note of number of alphabets written in 1 minute in Final activity 9 column of the table.

Activity 1 Initial time	Activity 2 Pangram	Activity 3 Alphabet Flow	Activity 4 Airbrushing			Activity 5 Table writing			Activity 6 Speed Pangram	Activity 7 Speed Writing	Activity 8 Challenge	**Final Activity 9 Jet Speed**
			A1	A2	A3	B1	B2	B3				__letters/ min

Compare the number of letters achieved in final activity 9 column with those in activity 1.

Even though a small difference is commendable! But on the contrary, you will be noticing a significant difference in the numbers and improvement in the speed of writing!

Congratulate yourself on achieving this new speed, as it represents your new speed of writing in terms of letters-per-minute rate.

Consistently performing the exercises outlined on the previous pages can gradually lead to a significant improvement in speed.

To further enhance your speed, try the Hack given next....

Now the question is how do we maintain this speed for future?

We will sharing a wonderful hack, which if followed religiously can give you tremendous results!

It's called '**The 15 Minutes Hack! '**

This technique involves allocating just 15 minutes each day to work on your notes. If you find that 15 minutes isn't enough, increase the time by 5 minutes, and aim to complete the task within this new 20-minute limit. If you still need more time, continue adding 5-minute increments until you find a duration that suits you.

Once you determine the optimal time for yourself, commit to sticking to it daily. Set a timer for this duration and stop working as soon as the timer goes off—this is a crucial rule of the technique. Within 2-3 days, you'll start to adapt, realizing that you need to complete your work within this set timeframe. This adjustment will help your brain and body work more efficiently, thereby improving your writing speed and making note taking less burdensome as it starts consuming less time. As a result, you'll be able to complete notes in school or university and perform better during exams.

How to Implement the Hack?

1. **Set a Timer**: Use a timer to strictly limit the note-taking session to 15 minutes, which helps in maintaining focus and preventing overextension.
2. **Choose a Consistent Time**: Try to practice at the same time every day to establish a routine.
3. **Evaluate Progress**: Periodically assess the improvements in speed and quality to stay motivated and adjust strategies if needed.

This can have significant psychological and practical benefits, particularly in developing speed and efficiency. Here's how this practice can be beneficial:

Psychological Benefits:

1. **Builds a Habit**: Allocating a specific time each day for a task helps in habit formation. Practising consistently will make hand muscles adapted to it and develop cognitive pathways that doesn't make the task as new burden and this writing speed comes out naturally over time.
2. **Changes Vision**: On allocating just 15 mins to yourself to complete a particular task, doesn't makes one feel as a long tiring task, it changes the vision of how one looks at it , like from' Tedious notes taking for hours to just a 15 mins task'
3. **Focused attention**: Aim to complete the task in stipulated time, keeps one focused avoiding any kind of distraction, it makes the task feel achievable as one has to focus only for short span of time.
4. **Positive Motivation**: Once as you start finishing the task in given set of time, it provides a sense of accomplishment, which gives a positive motivation to continue the practice.
5. **Reduces Procrastination**: Knowing that the task will only take a short amount of time, reduces the intention of procrastinating and finish it at once in short time.

Practical Benefits

1. Daily habit developed: Small practice sessions every day regulates a habit of writing daily and gradually improves the speed of writing as well.
2. Time Management: Some children find writing notes very time consuming and burdensome, by fixing the time to write for a little time every day, this problem is elevated, the children also learn to manage time.
   - By dedicating a short, consistent amount of time each day to note-taking, individuals can develop faster and more efficient note-taking skills, enhance their overall productivity, and build a positive habit that contributes to academic and professional success.